DOWN MEMORY LANE

Ye Olde
SWEET
SHOP

igloobooks

igloobooks

Published in 2015
by Igloo Books Ltd
Cottage Farm
Sywell
NN6 0BJ
www.igloobooks.com

Cover images: © Thinkstock / Getty

Food photography and recipe development:
© Stockfood, The Food Media Agency

GUA006 0715
2 4 6 8 10 9 7 5 3 1
ISBN 978-1-78440-856-5

Printed and manufactured in China

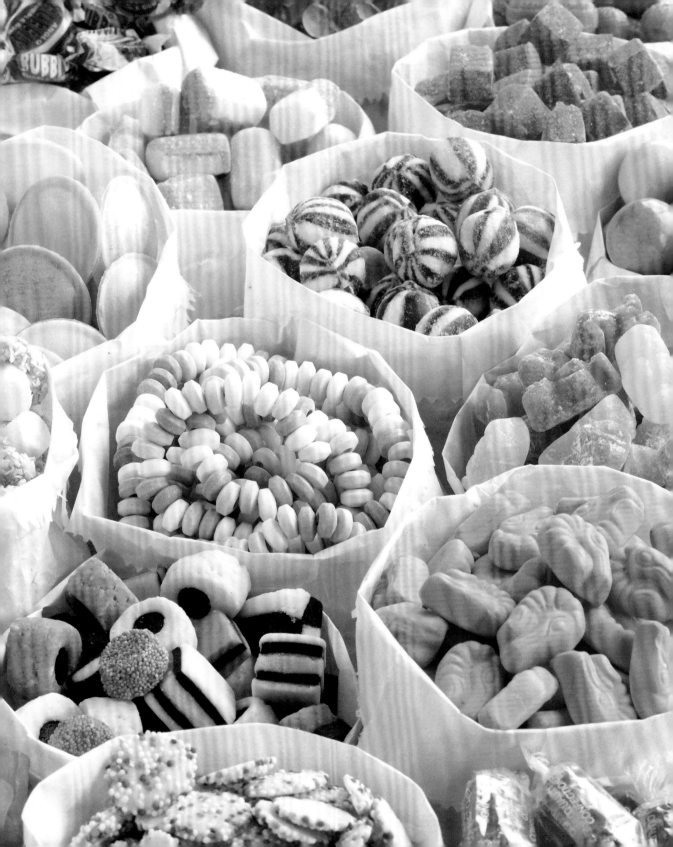

Contents

Introduction

Take a trip down memory lane with Ye Olde Sweet Shop - a vintage collection of sweetie recipes for kids and grown-ups, too!

This cookbook is filled with delicious confectionery that will delight and inspire cooks everywhere. It's bursting with scrumptious recipes that can be whipped up for special occasions and parties.

Sweet making doesn't have to be complicated - it can be fun! Ensure your kitchen is well-stocked with all the cooking essentials on our **Shopping List**, learn the science behind working with sugar and fill your cupboards with all the necessary ingredients. Once you've armed yourself with some handy tools, you'll be well on your way to candy-making success!

If it's a British classic sweet you're after, try the much-adored **Rhubarb Custards** - these hard-boiled candies make wonderful gifts. Learn how to dress-up your sweet creations with our **Gift Packaging** tips, packed full of decoration inspiration.

For fashionable candy, why not whip up a batch of bite-sized **French Macaroons**. These quintessentially French sweets are unique in their chewy texture and are guaranteed crowd-pleasers. There are plenty of sticky toffee treats, too. Try your hand at **Vanilla Tablet** and relish in the buttery, milky sweet experience. If you're playing party host, serve our delectable and boozy **Champagne Truffles** with your finest bubbly. Just make sure the kids don't get their hands on these adult treats!

At the end of the book you'll find **Nutritional Information** for each recipe. This guide lists the nutritional value of each sweet, so you can indulge in an informed manner.

Shopping List

Dairy and chocolate ingredients

Butter – fresh and unsalted, for greasing

Good-quality white, milk and dark chocolate (for best results, use dark chocolate with at least 60-68% cocoa content. Anything over will be bitter and overpower the other subtle ingredients)

Clotted cream

Cocoa butter

Cocoa powder

Condensed milk

Double (heavy) cream

Eggs – store at room temperature before use

Milk

Decorative ingredients

Assorted nuts

Candied mixed fruit

Coffee beans

Desiccated coconut

Dried fruit

Edible gold leaf

Glacé cherries

Oranges and lemons, for peel and zest

Extracts

Good-quality vanilla extract – and/ or other varieties such as lemon, peppermint, raspberry, strawberry

Rose water

Raising agents, thickening agents, setting agents and preservatives

Agar flakes (vegetarian friendly)

Bicarbonate of (baking) soda

Citric acid

Cornflour (cornstarch)

Cream of tartar

Gelatin sheets, granules and/or powder (fruity and plain)

Powdered jelly

Tartaric acid

Sugars and sweeteners

Caster (superfine) sugar

Corn syrup

Golden syrup

Granulated sugar

Honey

Icing (confectioners') sugar

Liquid glucose

Maple syrup

Other essentials

Clear piping gel

Food dye (natural and/or artificial)

Marzipan

Non-fat cooking spray, for greasing

Plain (all-purpose) flour

Ready-made fondant icing

Sunflower oil, for greasing

The Sweet Connoisseur's Toolbox

Sugar thermometers

Sugar thermometers measure the temperature of the sugar solution, which will indicate whether you are ready to move on to the next step of the recipe.

Brass thermometers are easily washable - no batteries are needed, so there are fewer components to wash. The digital models tend to read the temperature quicker and more accurately. Most thermometers are dishwasher friendly.

Top tip: Remember to calibrate your thermometer approximately every 4 or 5 times of use. Simply fill a saucepan with water and bring to boiling point. Once the water is boiling, check the temperature. It should read 100°C / 212F.

Chocolate tempering thermometers

The chocolate recipes in this book do not require a tempering thermometer. However, if you wish to use one in your truffle recipes this is not discouraged - they certainly are useful pieces of equipment to have in your culinary toolbox!

You can also use a digital probe sugar thermometer for your chocolate making. However, you must make sure that the thermometer is immaculately clean before use, to avoid cross-contamination. If there is any residue on the thermometer or spatula, this can spoil the mixture and upset the process.

Why temper?

Tempering your chocolate is a safe and foolproof approach that will guarantee a smooth and silky finish every time.

Chocolate contains fat, which is broken down in the cooking process and causes crystallisation. If the temperature is not controlled, the mixture can appear lumpy and inconsistent. To avoid this, it is recommended that the method be followed as accurately as possible with or without a chocolate thermometer.

Top tip: For precise temperature readings purchase a rubber spatula with a thermometer in the spoon. This way, the temperature will be measured straight from the mixture, instead of the bottom of the bowl.

Temperatures & Equipment

For chocolate tempering
Plain - 31-32°C (88-90F)
Milk - 30-31°C (86-88F)
White - 27-28°C (80-82F)

For sweets
Soft Ball (fudges and fondants)
   113-118°C (235-245F)
Hard Ball (marshmallows, caramels and nougats)
   118-130°C (245-266F)
Soft Crack (toffees and boiled sweets)
   132-143°C (270-290F)
Hard Crack (hard toffees) 149-154°C (300-310F)

Essential equipment
Baking tray
Greaseproof paper
Hand whisk
Heatproof bowl
Measuring spoons
Parchment paper
Plastic spatula
Solid-bottomed saucepan (to prevent sticking)
Wooden spoon - for toffee, nougat and fudge

Other
Chocolate and sweet moulds
Digital weighing scales
Dipping forks (for coating truffles)
Heat-resistant mat
Ice cream scoop (useful for truffles)
Lolly sticks
Palette knives (use in recipes that require a smooth finish, such as nougat, marshmallows and fudge)
Pastry scraper
Piping bag
Silicone baking mat
Sweet wrappers
Toffee hammer

Storing Sweets

When it comes to storage, each and every scrumptious recipe included in this book requires a certain amount of love and care. For those of you who are happy to devour the batch in one sitting, feel free to skip ahead to the recipes. But if you wish you give your sweet creations as a gift, or reserve a batch for the weekend, then read on.

Chocolate Truffles and Pralines

These sweets contain fresh cream so will need to be kept in the fridge in an airtight container. Consume within 3-4 days. If you decide to freeze a batch, they will last up to two months.

Coconut Ice

These treats have a slightly longer shelf life. They don't need to be kept in the fridge. For a tougher and chewier texture, keep cold. Store in an airtight container for up to one month.

Florentines

Store in an airtight container and consume within 2-3 days. For a more snappy chocolate these can be refrigerated, but be prepared for the dried fruit to harden slightly.

Fudge

These decadent treats contain dairy, so they need to be kept cold. Store in the fridge for up to two weeks or freeze for up to two months. Cut the fudge into squares before storing and allow it to warm to room temperature before serving.

Marshmallows

Unique in their fluffy, chewy texture, these treats are best eaten fresh. Ensure they are stored in an airtight container and separate each layer with parchment paper. They will last for up to four days.

Nougat

These treats also contain dairy and are similar to toffee in texture. For best results, store in a cool, dry place for up to four days.

Toffees and Caramels

The toffee recipes included in this book, including the Vanilla Tablet, should be stored in an airtight container to retain optimum quality and freshness. To avoid a sticky mess, wrap each individual sweet in parchment paper. They should last for up to one week.

Turkish Delight

Handle these sweets in a similar way to marshmallows. Store at room temperature in an airtight container, lined with parchment paper. To avoid them sticking together, dust each sweet with icing sugar and/or cornflour.

Gift Packaging

Home-made sweets make wonderful gifts and it's completely up to you how you wish to present them. For inspiration, collect magazines, old postcards and scraps of newspaper. Flick through the pages of cookbooks and visit old-fashioned sweet shops.

Gift packaging is totally affordable if you choose to make everything yourself. Here are some ideas that can be made in the home.

Jars, boxes, tins

It's important to think about storage when you package your sweets. If your gift needs to be kept refrigerated, it's best to store the sweets already wrapped in the fridge. Try to avoid the sweets being kept in a warm place for too long, as this may spoil them.

Sticky sweets such as caramel and toffee are best wrapped individually in parchment paper. These can then be wrapped in cellophane or left loose in a box or jam jar.

Chocolates, truffles and pralines are best presented in a box or tin. This will ensure they don't lose their shape. If you've made a big batch, use parchment paper to divide the layers so they don't stick to each other.

Gift tags

Any kind of consumable gift is almost always best presented with a gift tag, complete with the recipe title – this makes the present more personal for that special someone. You can have a bit of fun with this. Why not create a logo with your initials or give yourself a fun sweet shop name for novelty value!

Some people like to know the ingredients and nutritional information of the sweets they're consuming.

You could always include this on your gift tag, or write it on a piece of card to slip inside the box or jar of goodies.

If you're going for the rustic, hand-made look, you can buy plain brown labels from most stationary shops. Even better, why not make your own from an old shoebox or piece of scrap paper? When it comes to gift packaging, think re-use and recycle for originality. This way you can spend less on packaging and more on the ingredients, which is always preferable!

Finishing touches

This is where you can really get creative! For sweets wrapped in cellophane, you can add dried flowers, rose petals or confetti for a lovely, delicate touch. Boxes and jars can also be filled with pretty decorations, shredded paper or straw depending on the finish you want.

If you choose to make a gift tag, secure it using ribbon or string. For jars, boxes and tins, stick on some buttons in assorted sizes. They are quirky and fun, plus little ones will love to help you stick them on!

DOWN MEMORY LANE

BOILED
SWEETS &
SOFT
CANDIES

Lemon Drops

Makes: 24 drops   Preparation time: 20-25 minutes   Cooking time: 15 minutes

INGREDIENTS

225 g / 8 oz / 1 cup granulated sugar

110 ml / 4 fl. oz / ½ cup water

½ tsp cream of tartar

¾ tsp lemon extract

2 tsp citric acid

a few drops of natural yellow food dye

65 g / 2 ½ oz / ½ cup icing (confectioners')
    sugar

1 tbsp sunflower oil, for greasing

METHOD

• Heat together the granulated sugar, water and cream of tartar in a saucepan set over a moderate heat.

• Once the sugar has dissolved, increase the heat and boil the syrup until it registers 150°C / 300F on a sugar thermometer.

• Remove from the heat and pour onto a silicone baking mat placed on a baking tray.

• Add the lemon extract, citric acid and a few drops of dye, mixing into the syrup with an oiled spatula or pastry scraper.

• Once cool enough to handle, shape the syrup into a rope and place the icing sugar in a large mixing bowl.

• Oil a pair of kitchen scissors and cut the rope into 24 individual drops, letting them drop into the icing sugar.

• Working quickly, roll the drops between palms into ovals and dust again in icing sugar.

• Let the drops cool and harden before serving.

Rhubarb Custards

Makes: 60   Preparation time: 30 minutes   Cooking time: 10 minutes

INGREDIENTS

450 g / 1 lb / 2 cups caster (superfine) sugar, plus extra for dusting

150 ml / 5 fl. oz / ⅔ cup water

½ tsp cream of tartar

2 tsp liquid glucose

2 tsp tartaric acid

1 ½ tsp good-quality vanilla extract

a few drops of yellow food dye

a few drops of red food dye

sunflower oil, for greasing

METHOD

- Preheat the oven to 110°C (90°C fan) / 225F / gas ¼ and prepare an ice bath in a mixing bowl large enough to hold a large saucepan.
- Combine the sugar, water, cream of tartar and glucose in a large saucepan. Cook over a medium heat, stirring occasionally, until the sugar has dissolved.
- Increase the heat and boil the syrup until it reaches 143°C / 290F on a sugar thermometer.
- Remove the saucepan from the heat and stir in the tartaric acid. Place the saucepan in the ice bath briefly.
- Pour half of the syrup onto a silicone baking mat or a non-stick baking tray, then return the saucepan to a low heat.
- Using a pastry scraper, fold the vanilla extract and a few drops of yellow food dye into the syrup on the mat or tray, folding the edges inwards towards the centre and working the syrup into a cylinder shape.
- Take the ends of the cylinder and pull them together to form a 'U' shape. Twist together and rework into a cylinder.
- Repeat this step for 15 minutes. Briefly return the cylinder to the oven if it becomes too tough to handle.
- Once finished, place the cylinder in the oven. Pour the remaining syrup from the saucepan onto a clean silicone mat or non-stick baking tray.
- Work a few drops of red food dye into the syrup using the pastry scraper; leave to cool and firm up before shaping into a cylinder.
- Remove the prepared sugar from the oven and shape both yellow and pink strands to the same length.
- Tease them together using slightly dampened fingers, then oil a pair of scissors and cut the strand into 60 pieces.
- Roll into ovals between oiled palms before dusting with caster sugar. Leave to cool and harden before serving.

Jelly Beans

Makes: approx. 120 beans   Preparation time: 1 hours 45 minutes   Cooking time: 10-15 minutes

INGREDIENTS

225 g / 8 oz / 1 cup caster (superfine) sugar

1 tsp cornflour (cornstarch)

110 ml / 4 fl. oz / ½ cup water

1 tbsp liquid glucose

4 tsp raspberry extract

4 tsp lemon extract

a few drops of assorted natural food dyes
   (blue, yellow, green and red)

1 tbsp cocoa butter, grated

METHOD

• Combine the sugar and cornflour in a heavy-based saucepan.

• Whisk in the water and liquid glucose until smooth, then heat over a medium heat until the sugar dissolves.

• Increase the heat and bring the syrup to boiling point, cooking it until it registers 118°C / 245F.

• Working quickly, pour the sugar syrup into jelly bean moulds and then leave them to set for 1 hour.

• Turn out the beans and set to one side.

• Add 1 tsp of raspberry extract to two bowls and do the same with the lemon extract to leave you with four bowls of extract.

• Add drops of dye to each bowl, mix until evenly coated, then add a quarter of the beans to each bowl.

• Mix with a spoon to coat evenly, then remove them.

• Add 1 tsp of extract to each corresponding bowl and more food dye, mixing until even.

• Return the beans and mix thoroughly again with a spoon, until coated.

• Working in batches, tumble the beans with some grated cocoa butter in a rock tumbler until smooth for approximately 45 minutes, then serve.

Seaside Rock Lollies

Makes: 8   Preparation time: 20-25 minutes   Cooking time: 15-20 minutes

INGREDIENTS

450 g / 1 lb / 2 cups granulated sugar

75 g / 3 oz / ⅓ cup liquid glucose

150 ml / 5 fl. oz / ⅔ cup water

½ tsp cream of tartar

a few drops of peppermint oil or
    peppermint extract

a few drops of white food dye

a few drops of natural red food dye

1 tbsp sunflower oil, for greasing

METHOD

- Preheat the oven to its lowest heat.

- Heat together the sugar, glucose and water in a saucepan set over a moderate heat.

- Stir occasionally until the sugar dissolves, and then increase the heat and boil until the syrup registers 114°C / 237F on a sugar thermometer.

- Stir in the cream of tartar and continue to cook the syrup until it reaches 127°C / 260F.

- Add the peppermint extract, swirl briefly, and pour half into a second saucepan.

- Add a little white food dye to the first saucepan, then pour onto a silicone mat sat on top of a baking tray.

- Add a little red food dye to the second saucepan of syrup.

- Pour this mixture out onto a silicone mat sat on top of another large baking tray, and place in the oven.

- As the white syrup cools and hardens, oil a pastry scraper to bring the edges in towards the centre of the syrup.

- Once it is cool enough to handle, start to roll, pull and then fold the syrup back into itself.

- Continue in this fashion for a few minutes until you have an even white piece of syrup. Roll it into a cylinder and place it in the oven on a silicone mat.

- Remove the red syrup and repeat the rolling, pulling and folding process with it, until firm yet malleable.

- Cut both the white and red pieces of candy into four pieces and press them into each other, layering them alternately.

- Roll this piece into a cylinder on a silicone mat, and cut into four pieces as it reaches 2 cm (1 in) diameter.

- Cut each piece in half and whilst holding one end against the mat, lightly roll the other end to create a spiral pattern.

- Repeat for each rock lolly, leaving them to dry at room temperature before serving.

Peppermint Candy Canes

Makes: 16 canes   Preparation time: 40-50 minutes   Cooking time: 20 minutes

INGREDIENTS

500 g / 1 lb 2 oz / 2¼ cups caster (superfine) sugar

1½ tbsp distilled white vinegar

125 ml / 4½ fl. oz / ½ cup water

1 tsp peppermint extract

a few drops of natural red food dye

a few drops of natural white food dye

1 tbsp sunflower oil, for greasing

METHOD

• Preheat the oven to 110°C (90°C fan) / 225F / gas ¼ .

• Combine the sugar, vinegar and water in a heavy-based saucepan set over a medium heat.

• Cook until the sugar dissolves, then increase the heat until it reaches boiling point.

• Continue to boil until it registers 160°C / 320F on a sugar thermometer.

• Frequently brush down the insides of the saucepan with a pastry brush dipped in water.

• Divide the syrup by pouring onto two silicone baking mats.

• Add half the peppermint extract to each mat and then add the red dye to one and white to the other.

• Using an oiled pastry scraper, incorporate the extract and dye into the sugars by folding it inwards from the edges.

• Continue bringing the edges over and towards the centre of the mats as the sugars cool.

• Place the white sugar in the oven to keep warm.

• Pick up the other sugar and pull it between your hands until glossy, stretching it out into a long rope.

• Take the ends and bring them together, twisting the candy into a rope and stretching it out again.

• Repeat until the candy cools and is barely warm, then shape into a strand with a diameter of 5 cm (2 in).

• Place in the oven to keep warm and shape the white sugar into the same 5 cm (2 in) strand as you did with the red.

• Place the two strands together and cut into 16 6 cm (2½ in) segments, then return all but one segment to the oven.

• Roll the segment into a log, twisting and pulling into candy cane shapes.

• Repeat with the other segments and leave the canes to cool and harden at room temperature before serving.

Gum Drops

Makes: 80 drops   Preparation time: 1 hour 15 minutes   Cooking time: 15 minutes

INGREDIENTS

non-fat cooking spray

2 tbsp plain powdered gelatin

600 g / 1 lb 5 oz / 2 ½ cups granulated sugar

325 g / 11 oz / 1 ⅓ cups apple sauce

2 tsp lemon juice

100 g / 3 ½ oz / ⅔ cup fruity powdered
   gelatin (assorted kinds)

METHOD

• Grease four small baking tins with non-fat cooking spray.

• Divide the plain gelatin between four small saucepans and add 1 tbsp of water to each.

• Divide 500 g / 1 lb 2 oz / 2 ¼ cups of the sugar into four and add to the softened gelatin.

• Add a quarter of the apple sauce to each along with ½ tsp of lemon juice.

• Divide the fruity gelatin between each saucepan and stir well.

• Cook each over a moderate heat until boiling and then continue to cook for a further minute.

• Pour immediately into the prepared tins and chill for 1 hour until set.

• Loosen the set gelatin from the tins and turn out.

• Use a small cutter to stamp out drops before shaping and rolling in the remaining granulated sugar.

• Leave to set at room temperature before serving.

Turkish Delight

Makes: 32 pieces   Preparation time: 6 hours 20 minutes   Cooking time: 45-55 minutes

INGREDIENTS

275 g / 9 oz / 1 ¼ cups caster (superfine) sugar

85 g / 3 ½ oz / ⅓ cup honey

350 ml / 12 fl. oz / 1 ½ cups water

¾ tsp cream of tartar

150 g / 5 oz / 1 cup cornflour (cornstarch)

175 g / 6 oz / 1 ½ cups icing (confectioners') sugar, sifted

1 ½ tsp rose water

a few drops of natural red food dye

1 ½ tsp lemon extract

a few drops of natural yellow food dye

METHOD

- Grease and line the base and sides of two 18 cm x 18 cm x 6 cm (7 in x 7 in x 2 ½ in) baking tins with greaseproof paper.
- Combine the caster sugar, honey, 55 ml / 2 fl. oz / ¼ cup of water and ½ tsp of cream of tartar in a saucepan set over a medium heat.
- Cook until the sugar and honey have dissolved, and then increase the heat until the syrup reaches boiling point.
- Cook until it registers 127°C / 260F on a sugar thermometer, approximately 8-10 minutes.
- In the meantime, combine half of the cornflour with the remaining water, as well as 65 g / 2 ½ oz / ⅔ cup of icing sugar and the remaining cream of tartar in a saucepan.
- As the sugar syrup reaches 120°C / 248F, start to cook the cornflour mixture for 2-3 minutes over a medium heat, until thickened, and then remove from the heat.
- Once the sugar syrup reaches 127°C / 260F, carefully whisk it off the heat into the cornflour mixture.
- Return the mixture to a medium-low heat and cook for 25-35 minutes, stirring frequently, until light golden and glue-like in consistency.
- Divide the mixture between the tins and add rose water and red dye to one and lemon and yellow dye to the other.
- Mix well and then cover the surfaces with a piece of cling film.
- Leave to cool and set for 6 hours or overnight.
- Whisk together the remaining cornflour and icing sugar in a large mixing bowl.
- Turn out the Turkish delight and cut into cubes. Evenly coat in the cornflour and icing sugar and then serve.

Fruit Jellies

Makes: 200 jellies   Preparation time: 2 hours 20-25 minutes   Cooking time: 20 minutes

INGREDIENTS

125 ml / 4 ½ fl. oz / ½ cup apple juice

a few drops of natural green food dye

125 ml / 4 ½ fl. oz / ½ cup orange cordial

a few drops of natural orange food dye

125 ml / 4 ½ fl. oz / ½ cup lemon cordial

a few drops of natural yellow food dye

125 ml / 4 ½ fl. oz / ½ cup raspberry cocktail juice

600 ml / 1 pint 2 fl. oz / 2 ½ cups water

2 tbsp citric acid, plus an extra 1 tbsp to finish

175 g / 6 oz / 1 cup powdered gelatin

675 g / 1 lb 8 oz / 3 cups caster (superfine) sugar

55 g / 2 oz / ¼ cup granulated sugar

METHOD

• Place the apple juice in a small saucepan and add a few drops of green food dye.

• Do the same with the orange cordial and the orange food dye, as well as the lemon cordial and yellow food dye.

• Place the raspberry cocktail juice in a fourth saucepan and set them to one side.

• Add 75 ml / 3 fl. oz / ⅓ cup of water to each saucepan and stir well.

• Add ½ tbsp of citric acid to each, stir well, and then sprinkle a quarter of the gelatin over each.

• Leave them to sit undisturbed for 15 minutes.

• Combine the sugar with the remaining water in a large saucepan and cook over a moderate heat until the sugar has dissolved.

• Increase the heat and continue to cook until the syrup registers 149°C / 300F on a sugar thermometer.

• Working quickly, whisk one quarter of the hot syrup into each saucepan of flavouring.

• Place the four saucepans over a low heat and cook for 2-3 minutes, stirring frequently, making sure that the mixtures don't boil.

• Pour the syrups into silicone sweet or candy moulds and leave them to set for 2 hours, covered loosely, at room temperature.

• Turn out the jellies onto a piece of greaseproof paper and mix the granulated sugar with 1 tbsp of citric acid.

• Working in batches, toss each variety of jelly in the mixture to coat.

• Leave them to rest uncovered overnight before serving.

Marshmallows

Makes: approx. 120 marshmallows   Preparation time: 2 hours 15 minutes   Cooking time: 20-25 minutes

INGREDIENTS

2 tbsp powdered gelatin

275 ml / 10 fl. oz / 1 ¼ cups water

450 g / 1 lb / 2 cups granulated sugar

1 ½ tsp vanilla extract

1 tbsp sunflower oil, for greasing

65 g / 2 ½ oz / ½ cup icing (confectioners') sugar

55 g / 2 oz / ¼ cup cornflour (cornstarch)

a few drops of natural red food dye

a few drops of natural yellow food dye

a few drops of natural green food dye

METHOD

• Place the gelatin and 2 tbsp of water in a heatproof bowl, then leave the gelatin to soften for 10 minutes.

• Meanwhile, combine the sugar with the remaining water in a large saucepan set over a moderate heat.

• Cook until the sugar has dissolved, stirring frequently.

• Bring the sugar to a boil and then reduce to a simmer until the sugar registers 113˚C / 235F on a sugar thermometer.

• Use an electric mixer to gradually beat the sugar syrup into the gelatin mixture.

• Add the vanilla extract and continue to beat for 15-18 minutes until the mixture is thick, cool and setting.

• Grease and line four small baking tins with greaseproof paper and grease with a little sunflower oil.

• Combine the icing sugar and cornflour and lightly dust the insides of the tins with the mixture.

• Working quickly, divide the marshmallow mixture into four bowls and add the dye to each of the three bowls, leaving the fourth white.

• Pour the pink marshmallow mixture into one tin, the green into another, the yellow into a third and the white into the fourth.

• Smooth the tops of the marshmallow mixtures with a damp palette knife before dusting with a little more icing sugar and cornflour.

• Cover with cling film and leave the marshmallows to set in a cool, dry place for 1 hour.

• Once set, use a small circular cutter to cut out marshmallows from the tins.

• Dust with more icing sugar and cornflour before serving.

Strawberry Laces

Makes: 24 laces   Preparation time: 2 hours 10 minutes   Cooking time: 10 minutes

INGREDIENTS

non-fat cooking spray

¾ tsp citric acid

55 g / 2 oz / ¼ cup caster (superfine) sugar

125 ml / 4 ½ fl. oz / ½ cup water

2 tbsp powdered gelatin

110 g / 4 oz / ½ cup granulated sugar

1 tsp natural strawberry extract

METHOD

- Spray the insides of lace candy moulds with non-fat cooking spray and combine ½ tsp of citric acid with the caster sugar.

- Dust the moulds with half of the sugar, tipping out the excess.

- Combine 2 tbsp of water with the gelatin in a small mixing bowl.

- Combine the remaining water with the granulated sugar in a small saucepan and cook over a low heat until the sugar dissolves.

- Warm the gelatin mixture in a microwave for 10-15 seconds until liquid.

- Add the gelatin to the sugar syrup and stir together off the heat.

- Add the **strawberry extract** and ¼ tsp of citric acid, stirring to combine, and then pour into a jug with a small spout.

- Pour the mixture into the moulds and dust with the remaining caster sugar mixture.

- Let the laces stand and dry at room temperature before turning out and serving.

Candied Fruit

Makes: 60 pieces   Preparation time: 1 hours 30 minutes   Cooking time: 15 minutes

INGREDIENTS

175 g / 6 oz / ¾ cup pectin sugar

175 ml / 6 fl. oz / ¾ cup water

½ tsp bicarbonate of (baking) soda

350 g / 12 oz / 1 ½ cups caster (superfine) sugar

225 g / 8 oz / 1 cup light corn syrup

1 tsp lemon extract

1 tsp orange extract

a few drops of natural orange food dye

a few drops of natural yellow food dye

white icing pen

METHOD

• Grease and line two small square baking tins with greaseproof paper.

• Combine the pectin sugar, water, and bicarbonate of soda in a saucepan.

• Combine 225 g / 8 oz / 1 cup of the caster sugar with the corn syrup in another saucepan.

• Cook both saucepans over a moderate heat for 4 minutes, stirring occasionally, until the foam has thinned out from the pectin mixture and the sugar and corn syrup mixture is at boiling point.

• Gradually whisk the pectin mixture into the sugar syrup until incorporated.

• Cook at a boil for one minute, and then pour half into another saucepan.

• Add the extracts to each mixture and dye appropriately with a few drops of the dye.

• Pour the mixtures into the prepared tins and leave to stand at room temperature overnight.

• Turn out the candies and dust with half of the remaining sugar. Use a small round cutter to cut out rounds of candy.

• Cut the rounds in half to make the citrus slices, and use a white icing pen to draw on the pith.

• Leave the candies to set for an hour, then roll in the remaining sugar to coat.

• Leave to set at room temperature overnight, then serve.

Berry Jellies

Makes: 24   Preparation time: 1 hour 20 minutes   Cooking time: 15 minutes   Setting time: 4 days

INGREDIENTS

non-fat cooking spray

125 g / 4 ½ oz / 1 cup icing (confectioners')
  sugar

55 g / 2 oz / ¼ cup cornflour (cornstarch)

½ tsp gum arabic

450 g / 1 lb / 2 cup caster (superfine) sugar

225 g / 8 oz / 1 cup liquid glucose

125 ml / 4 ½ fl. oz / ½ cup water

½ tsp blackberry extract

½ tsp raspberry extract

½ tsp strawberry extract

½ tsp blackcurrant extract

a few drops of natural red food dye

a few drops of natural purple food dye

METHOD

- Spray the insides of a candy mould with non-fat cooking spray.

- Mix together the icing sugar and cornflour in a shaker and then dust the insides of the moulds with the mixture, making two passes.

- Stir together the gum arabic and 1 tbsp of water in a small bowl until dissolved. Set to one side for 1 hour.

- Combine the caster sugar, glucose and water in a saucepan and cook over a moderate heat until the sugar dissolves.

- Brush down the sides of the saucepan with a wetted pastry brush if needed.

- Cook until the mixture registers 110°C / 230F on a sugar thermometer and then remove it from the heat and stir in the gum arabic mixture.

- Divide the mixture between four saucepans.

- Add individual fruit extract to each saucepan and then add the corresponding dyes, swirling until even in appearance.

- Carefully pour the syrups into the candy moulds and dust the tops with another pass of icing sugar and cornflour.

- Leave the jellies to dry out at room temperature for at least four days before turning out and serving.

Orange, Lemon & Lime Drops

Makes: 36   Preparation time: 30-35 minutes   Cooking time: 15-20 minutes

INGREDIENTS

900 g / 2 lb / 4 cups caster (superfine) sugar

3 tbsp distilled vinegar

300 ml / 10 ½ fl. oz / 1 ⅓ cups water

½ tsp lime extract

½ tsp lemon extract

½ tsp orange extract

½ tsp aniseed or liquorice extract

a few drops of liquid food dye (green, yellow, and orange)

a little sunflower oil, for greasing

METHOD

- Preheat the oven to 130°C (110°C fan) / 250F / gas ½ .

- Combine the sugar, vinegar and water in a large saucepan and cook over a moderate heat until it reaches 160°C / 320F on a sugar thermometer.

- If needed, brush down the sides of the saucepan with a wetted pastry brush to prevent crystallisation.

- Divide the cooked sugar evenly by pouring onto five individual silicone mats.

- Add a few drops of lime extract and green dye to one, lemon and yellow to a second, orange extract and dye to a third and aniseed to the fourth. Leave the fifth plain.

- Using an oiled spatula or knife, gently fold the dye and extract into the sugars. Place four of the mats in the oven to keep warm as you work with the fifth.

- Fold the sugar onto itself as it cools, pulling and folding continuously until uniform and even.

- Repeat this step with each piece of sugar, working them until even and glossy, and then placing them back in the oven to keep warm.

- Fold and pull the final batch of sugar until it starts to turn white.

- Cut the white sugar into four pieces and place back in the oven until malleable and easy to shape.

- Working one by one, thinly roll out the white sugar into a long strip before draping back and forth over a fruity piece to cover.

- Lift the middle of the fruity sugar up, letting the two ends meet before folding onto itself.

- Roll into a rough cigar shape and cut into odd shapes using a pair of oiled scissors.

- Repeat with the other extracts and then leave the candies to cool and harden before serving.

Peppermint Creams

Makes: 32 creams   Preparation time: 2 hours 20 minutes

INGREDIENTS

450 g / 1 lb / 4 cups icing (confectioners')
    sugar, plus extra for dusting
225 g / 8 oz / 1 cup condensed milk
a few drops of peppermint extract
a few drops of natural white food dye

METHOD

• Sift the icing sugar into a large mixing bowl.

• Gradually whisk the condensed milk into the sugar, mixing until evenly smooth.

• Add the peppermint extract and a few drops of food dye, kneading well to
  incorporate.

• Turn out the dough onto a surface dusted with icing sugar and knead briefly.

• Roll it out to 0.5 mm (¼ in) thickness and use a small straight-sided cutter to stamp
  out rounds.

• Use the tip of a cake tester to decorate their tops with small circles.

• Leave the creams to dry and set for 2 hours before serving.

Liquorice Sticks

Makes: 32 sticks   Preparation time: 40-45 minutes   Cooking time: 15 minutes

INGREDIENTS

75 g / 3 oz / ½ cup plain (all-purpose flour), sifted

a pinch of salt

110 g / 4 oz / ½ cup unsalted butter, softened

200 g / 7 oz / 1 cup caster (superfine) sugar

175 g / 6 oz / ¾ cup light corn syrup

85 g / 3 ½ oz / ⅓ cup golden syrup

¾ tsp strawberry extract

a few drops of natural red food dye

METHOD

• Grease and line the base and sides of a 23 cm x 23 cm x 6 cm (9 in x 9 in x 2 ½ in) baking tin with greaseproof paper.

• Whisk together the flour and salt in a small mixing bowl, setting it to one side.

• Combine the butter, sugar, corn syrup and golden syrup in a saucepan.

• Cook over a medium heat, stirring, until the sugar has dissolved.

• Increase the heat and boil until the syrup registers 116°C / 240F on a sugar thermometer.

• Remove the syrup from the heat and beat in the flour mixture, working quickly and efficiently.

• Add the extract and a few drops of dye, mixing well, until red.

• Pour into the prepared tin and cover and chill for 30 minutes.

• Carefully turn out the sheet of licorice and place on a flat cutting board.

• Cut in half with a sharp chef's knife and then slice each half into 0.5 cm (¼ in) strips.

• Twist the ends of the strips in opposite directions to create spirals.

• Leave them to set at room temperature before serving.

Soft Nougat Squares

Makes: 16 squares   Preparation time: 1 hour   Cooking time: 20-25 minutes

INGREDIENTS

225 g / 8 oz / 1 cup caster (superfine) sugar

125 g / 4 ½ oz / ½ cup liquid glucose

55 ml / 2 fl. oz / ¼ cup water

3 large egg whites

1 tsp vanilla extract

2 tbsp cherry jam (jelly)

2 tbsp caramel sauce

2 tbsp chocolate syrup

2 tbsp shredded coconut

METHOD

- Combine the sugar, glucose and water in a saucepan, cooking them over a medium heat until the sugar has dissolved.

- Increase the heat and boil the syrup, undisturbed, until it starts to approach 114°C / 237F on a sugar thermometer.

- Beat the egg whites in a heatproof mixing bowl for 1 minute until frothy.

- Continue to cook the syrup until it reaches 118°C / 245F and remove it from the heat.

- Pour a little of the syrup into the whites and beat to incorporate.

- Slowly beat in the remaining syrup and continue for 2-3 minutes until thick and frothy.

- Add the vanilla extract and continue to beat for a further 3 minutes until stiffly peaked.

- Divide the mixture evenly between three bowls, swirling cherry jam into one and caramel sauce into another.

- Fully incorporate the chocolate sauce into the third.

- Grease and line three small, square baking tins with greaseproof paper.

- Scrape the mixtures into each tin and smooth the top with a wetted spoon.

- Sprinkle the coconut over half of the chocolate mixture and leave the sweets to cool to room temperature.

- Turn them out and cut into squares before serving.

DOWN MEMORY LANE

CARAMEL,
TOFFEE &
FUDGE

Salted Butter Toffees

Makes: 48   Preparation time: 3 hour 20 minutes   Cooking time: 15-20 minutes

INGREDIENTS

150 ml / 5 fl. oz / ⅔ cup double (heavy) cream
55 g / 2 oz / ¼ cup salted butter, cubed
½ tsp vanilla extract
2 tsp flaked sea salt
150 g / 5 oz / ½ cup golden syrup
225 g / 8 oz / 1 cup caster (superfine) sugar

METHOD

- Grease and line a 20 cm (8 in) square baking tin with greaseproof paper.

- Heat the cream with 2 tbsp of the butter, the vanilla extract and half of the salt.

- Once the mixture starts to boil, remove it from the heat and keep it warm to one side.

- Cook the golden syrup with the sugar in a large, heavy-based saucepan, until it registers 155°C / 310F on a sugar thermometer.

- Turn off the heat under the saucepan and stir through the warm cream.

- Once the cream has been incorporated, warm it over a moderate heat until it registers 127°C / 260F on the thermometer.

- Remove the caramel from the heat and stir in the remaining butter until incorporated.

- Sprinkle the remaining salt over the base of the lined baking tin and pour the hot caramel over it.

- Leave it to cool and set at room temperature for approximately 3 hours.

- Once cool, remove the set toffee and cut into cubes before serving.

Vanilla Tablet

Makes: 32 pieces   Preparation time: 40 minutes   Cooking time: 35-45 minutes

INGREDIENTS

2 tbsp unsalted butter, softened

150 ml / 5 fl. oz / ⅔ cup whole milk

500 g / 1 lb 2 oz / 2 ¼ cups granulated sugar

400 g / 14 oz / 2 cups condensed milk

1 tsp vanilla extract

METHOD

- Grease and line a 20 cm (8 in) square baking tin with greaseproof paper. Grease the paper with butter.

- Stir together the milk, sugar, and condensed milk in a large, heavy-based saucepan, and cook over a low heat for 20-25 minutes until thickened.

- Once thickened and light brown in appearance, stir in the vanilla extract.

- Remove from the heat and beat well with a spoon for 10-15 minutes until the mixture starts to come away from the base and sides of the pan.

- Pour into the prepared tin and leave it to cool for 20 minutes.

- Turn out the set tablet and break into pieces.

- Leave to cool for a further 10 minutes before serving.

Toffee

Makes: 16 pieces   Preparation time: 2 hours 10 minutes   Cooking time: 20 minutes

INGREDIENTS

175 g / 6 oz / ¾ cup unsalted butter

225 g / 8 oz / 1 cup caster (superfine) sugar

2 tbsp water

1 tsp vanilla extract

METHOD

- Grease and line a large baking tray with a sheet of greaseproof paper.

- Combine the butter, sugar and water in a large saucepan set over a medium heat.

- Cook until the sugar dissolves, stirring from time to time.

- Increase the heat and boil the toffee until it registers 150°C / 302F on a sugar thermometer.

- Remove the toffee from the heat and carefully swirl in the vanilla extract.

- Pour the toffee onto the prepared tray and leave it to set and cool.

- Once cool, break into pieces and serve.

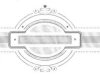

Salted Caramels

Makes: 12   Preparation time: 45–50 minutes   Cooking time: 15 minutes

INGREDIENTS

225 g / 8 oz / 1 cup granulated sugar

110 g / 4 oz / ½ cup salted butter, cubed

125 ml / 4 ½ fl. oz / ½ cup whipping cream

½ tsp salt, to taste

450 g / 1 lb / 3 cups 70% cocoa dark
    chocolate, chopped

non-fat cooking spray

METHOD

- Cook the granulated sugar in a saucepan set over a moderate heat until dissolved and golden.

- Add the butter, cube by cube, and continue to cook for 3 minutes over a reduced heat until incorporated.

- Whisk in the cream in a slow, steady stream and cook the sauce at a boil for a further minute.

- Remove it from the heat and season to taste with salt.

- Set the sauce to one side to cool and thicken.

- Place the chocolate in a food processor and blitz until it resembles breadcrumbs.

- Meanwhile, fill a large bowl with boiling water and set to one side.

- Scrape down the sides of the food processor bowl and continue to blitz for a further 2 minutes until the chocolate starts to clump into a ball.

- Break up the ball with a spatula and scrape it down into the base of the bowl.

- Blitz the chocolate again until it starts to liquefy and registers 32°C / 90F on a sugar thermometer.

- Pour the water out of the warm bowl and dry it thoroughly. Scrape the liquid chocolate into the warmed bowl and stir until even and fluid.

- Lightly spray the insides of a 12-hole chocolate mould with cooking spray.

- Fill each hole with tempered chocolate and tap lightly to release trapped air bubbles.

- Invert the mould over a large bowl, resting its ends over it, so that most of the chocolate runs into the bowl.

- Set the mould on a level tray and chill for 10 minutes until set.

- Remove the mould and fill the shells with the caramel, stopping short of their tops.

- Gently tap them to release any air and chill for 5 minutes.

- Warm the tempered chocolate back to 32°C / 90F over a bain-marie. Spoon it over the filled shells and chill for 10 minutes.

- Carefully turn out the chocolates and clean their edges with a sharp paring knife before serving.

Butterscotch Fudge

Makes: 32 pieces   Preparation time: 1 hour 10 minutes   Cooking time: 10-15 minutes

INGREDIENTS

1 tbsp sunflower oil

225 g / 8 oz / 1 cup caster (superfine) sugar

100 g / 3 ½ oz / ⅓ cup golden syrup

225 g / 8 oz / 1 cup clotted cream

½ tsp vanilla extract

METHOD

- Grease and line the base and sides of a 18 cm (7 in) square baking tin with greaseproof paper.
- Brush the paper with sunflower oil and set it to one side.
- Combine the remaining ingredients in a large saucepan and cook over a medium heat until the sugar dissolves.
- Continue to cook over an increased heat, without stirring, until the mixture registers 116 °C / 240F on a sugar thermometer.
- Remove it from the heat and beat vigorously for 8-10 minutes until thick and slightly grainy.
- Pour it into the prepared tin and leave it to set at room temperature for up to an hour.
- Once set, turn out the fudge and cut into squares before serving.

Caramel Chews

Makes: 32   Preparation time: 2 hours 15 minutes   Cooking time: 20-25 minutes

INGREDIENTS

250 ml / 9 fl. oz / 1 cup double (heavy) cream
55 g / 2 oz / ¼ cup unsalted butter, softened
a pinch of salt
350 g / 12 oz / 1 ½ cups caster (superfine)
    sugar
75 g / 3 oz / ¼ cup golden syrup
55 g / 2 oz / ¼ cup water
½ tsp vanilla extract

METHOD

• Grease and line the base and sides of a 20 cm (8 in) square baking tin with greaseproof paper.

• Combine the cream and butter in a large saucepan and cook over a medium heat until melted together.

• Set to one side and carefully stir together the sugar, golden syrup and water in a large saucepan until smooth and even.

• Cook the mixture without touching until it registers 132°C / 270F on a sugar thermometer.

• Remove the sugar syrup from the heat and carefully whisk in the cream mixture.

• Return the caramel to a medium heat and cook until it registers 118°C / 245F.

• Whisk in the vanilla extract and pour the caramel into the prepared tin.

• Leave the caramel to set for 2 hours or overnight.

• Lift the caramel out of the tin and cut into chews before wrapping in cellophane wrappers.

Cassis Cream Fudge

Makes: 24 pieces   **Preparation time:** 2 hours 20 minutes   **Cooking time:** 15-20 minutes

INGREDIENTS

450 g / 1 lb / 2 cups caster (superfine) sugar
110 ml / 4 fl. oz / ½ cup whole milk
75 g / 3 oz / ⅓ cup double (heavy) cream
2 tbsp golden syrup
75 g / 3 oz / ⅓ cup crème de cassis

METHOD

• Grease and line the base and sides of an 18 cm (7 in) square baking tin with greaseproof paper.

• Combine the sugar, milk, cream, and golden syrup in a large saucepan.

• Cook over a medium heat until the sugar dissolves.

• Continue to cook over an increased heat until the mixture registers 115°C / 239F on a sugar thermometer.

• Remove the mixture from the heat and scrape it into a bowl, leaving it to cool for 10 minutes.

• After cooling, beat with an electric whisk for 3 minutes until thick and matte in appearance.

• Add the crème de cassis and swirl it into the fudge with a cake tester or thin spatula before pouring it into the prepared tin.

• Leave it to set at room temperature for 2 hours, then turn out and cut into squares.

Chocolate & Vanilla Fudge

Makes: 48 pieces   Preparation time: 3 hours 15-25 minutes   Cooking time: 15 minutes

INGREDIENTS

450 g / 1 lb / 2 cups golden caster (superfine)
  sugar
400 ml / 14 fl. oz / 1 ¾ cups double (heavy)
  cream
55 g / 2 oz / ¼ cup unsalted butter, softened
1 tbsp liquid glucose
1 tsp vanilla extract
a pinch of salt
200 g / 7 oz / 1 ⅓ cups dark chocolate, finely
  chopped

METHOD

• Line the base and sides of a 20 cm x 10 cm x 6 cm (8 in x 4 in x 2 ½ in) baking tin with greaseproof paper.

• Combine the sugar, cream, butter and liquid glucose in a large saucepan, stirring well.

• Cook over a medium heat, stirring frequently, until the sugar dissolves.

• Increase the heat slightly until the syrup starts to boil.

• Once the syrup reaches 116°C / 240F on a sugar thermometer, remove the syrup from the heat.

• Leave it to stand for 5 minutes or until the temperature drops to 110°C / 230F, then stir in the vanilla extract and a pinch of salt.

• Beat the fudge thoroughly with a wooden spoon as it cools and drops to 60°C / 140F.

• Continue to beat firmly for 2 minutes, then pour half into the prepared tin.

• Working quickly, sprinkle over the chocolate and pour the rest of the fudge on top.

• Leave the fudge to cool and set until firm at room temperature.

• Turn out the fudge and cut into squares before serving.

Peanut Butter Fudge

Makes: 32 pieces   Preparation time: 2 hours 10-15 minutes   Cooking time: 15-20 minutes

INGREDIENTS

225 g / 8 oz / 1 cup unsalted butter

225 g / 8 oz / 1 cup smooth peanut butter

1 tsp vanilla extract

450 g / 1 lb / 4 cups icing (confectioners') sugar

150 g / 5 oz / 1 cup dark chocolate, chopped

1 tsp liquid glucose

100 g / 3 ½ oz / ¾ cup salted peanuts, crushed

METHOD

• Grease and line the base and sides of a 20 cm (8 in) square baking tin with greaseproof paper.

• Combine the butter and peanut butter in a saucepan and cook over a medium heat until melted together.

• Stir in the vanilla extract and icing sugar, away from the heat, until you have a thick, matte fudge mixture.

• Pour and scrape into the prepared tin. Cover the surface of the fudge with a sheet of greaseproof paper.

• Chill for 2 hours until set.

• After 2 hours, melt together the chocolate and liquid glucose in a heatproof bowl set over a half-filled saucepan of simmering water.

• Stir until melted before scraping into a piping bag fitted with a small, straight-sided nozzle.

• Turn out the fudge and cut into 2 cm (1 in) squares.

• Pipe the chocolate on top and sprinkle over some crushed peanuts.

• Leave the fudge to cool and set before serving.

Chocolate-coated Honeycomb

Makes: 6-8 pieces   Preparation time: 2 hours   Cooking time: 15-20 minutes

INGREDIENTS

non-stick cooking spray

450 g / 1 lb / 3 cups good-quality milk
  chocolate, chopped

225 g / 8 oz / 1 cup caster (superfine) sugar

75 g / 3 oz / ¼ cup golden syrup

2 tsp bicarbonate of (baking) soda

METHOD

• Grease and line the base and sides of a 20 cm (8 in) square springform baking tin with greaseproof paper.

• Spray the paper with non-fat cooking spray and set it to one side.

• Melt half of the chocolate in a heatproof bowl set over a saucepan of gently simmering water.

• Stir until melted and then pour the mixture into the lined baking tin. Place in the freezer for 20 minutes.

• After 20 minutes, cook the sugar and golden syrup in a saucepan set over a medium heat, without stirring.

• Once the sugar has dissolved continue to cook it for 3 minutes.

• Remove the saucepan from the heat and carefully whisk in the bicarbonate of soda.

• Once the honeycomb mixture bubbles down, pour it over the frozen chocolate and leave it to cool for 1 hour.

• Melt the remaining chocolate as before and leave it to cool and thicken slightly. Carefully pour the mixture over the set honeycomb.

• Chill for 30 minutes until set. Turn out from the tin and cut into pieces, then serve.

Chocolate & Coconut Fudge

Makes: 32 pieces   Preparation time: 2 hours 15 minutes   Cooking time: 15 minutes

INGREDIENTS

500 g / 1 lb 2 oz / 3 ⅓ cups dark chocolate, finely chopped

400 g / 14 oz / 1 ¾ cups condensed milk

2 tbsp unsalted butter

100 g / 3 ½ oz / ¾ cup icing (confectioners') sugar, sifted

a little extra icing (confectioners') sugar, for dusting

55 g / 2 oz / ⅔ cup desiccated coconut

METHOD

• Grease and line the base and sides of an 18 cm (7 in) square baking tin with greaseproof paper.

• Combine the chocolate, condensed milk and butter in a saucepan and heat gently. Stir well until smooth and silky.

• Stir in the icing sugar and the desiccated coconut and mix well.

• Press into the prepared tin and smooth the top with the back of a wetted tablespoon.

• Chill for 2 hours or until set.

• Turn out the fudge and cut into squares.

• Dust lightly with icing sugar before serving.

DOWN MEMORY LANE

NUTTY
SWEETS &
COCONUT
TREATS

Almond Hearts

Makes: 48   Preparation time: 50 minutes

INGREDIENTS

350 g / 12 oz / 3 cups ground almonds

375 g / 13 oz / 3 cups icing (confectioners')
  sugar, sifted

a little extra icing (confectioners') sugar,
  for dusting

2 tsp almond extract

1 small egg white

350 g / 12 oz / 1 ½ cups white fondant icing

METHOD

• Pulse together the ground almonds and icing sugar in a food processor until combined.

• Add the almond extract, pulse again, and then add the egg white.

• Process until a dough comes together.

• Turn out the dough and knead gently for a minute until smooth.

• Wrap in cling film and chill for 30 minutes.

• Turn out the almond paste onto a surface dusted with icing sugar.

• Roll to 2 cm (1 in) thickness and use a heart-shaped cutter to cut out hearts.

• Place the fondant icing in a mixing bowl and thin out with a little hot water, mixing gently with a spatula until spreadable.

• Brush the tops of the hearts with the icing, leaving them to set before serving.

Fruit & Nut Florentines

Makes: 24   Preparation time: 45-50 minutes   Cooking time: 10-12 minutes

INGREDIENTS

175 g / 6 oz / ¾ cup caster (superfine) sugar

110 g / 4 oz / ½ cup unsalted butter, cubed

75 g / 3 oz / ⅓ cup double (heavy) cream

2 tbsp honey

175 g / 6 oz / 1 ½ cups flaked (slivered) almonds

2 tbsp plain (all-purpose) flour

2 tbsp rolled oats

1 tsp freshly grated lemon zest

1 tbsp chopped mixed peel

75 g / 3 oz / 1 cup shredded coconut

100 g / 3 ½ oz / ⅔ cup glacé cherries, chopped

300 g / 10 ½ oz / 2 cups dark chocolate, chopped

1 tsp liquid glucose

METHOD

- Preheat the oven to 180°C (160°C fan) / 350F / gas 4.

- Grease and line a large baking tray with greaseproof paper.

- Heat together the sugar, butter, cream and honey in a large saucepan set over a moderate heat.

- Remove the saucepan from the heat and stir through the almonds, flour, oats, lemon zest, mixed peel, shredded coconut and half of the cherries.

- Leave the mixture to cool for 15 minutes before taking tablespoons of the batter and spooning mounds onto the prepared tray.

- Flatten the mounds with a wetted finger and bake for 10-12 minutes until golden on top.

- Remove the tray from the oven and leave to cool on a wire rack.

- Melt together the chocolate and glucose in a heatproof bowl set over a half-filled saucepan of simmering water.

- Stir until melted before removing from the heat.

- Carefully peel away the Florentines from the tray and dip their undersides in the melted chocolate.

- Chill the dipped Florentines on a wire rack, with the chocolate-side facing up, for 15 minutes.

- Garnish with the remaining chopped cherries before serving.

French Macaroons

Makes: 24   Preparation time: 45-50 minutes   Cooking time: 8-10 minutes

INGREDIENTS

750 g / 1 lb 10 oz / 6 cups icing (confectioners')
    sugar, sifted

350 g / 12 oz / 3 cups ground almonds

4 medium egg whites

a pinch of salt

½ tsp natural red food dye

½ tsp natural orange food dye

½ tsp natural green food dye

2 tsp almond extract

1 tbsp cocoa powder

2 tbsp hazelnuts (cobnuts), chopped

150 ml / 5 fl. oz / ⅔ cup double (heavy) cream

150 g / 5 oz / 1 cup dark chocolate, chopped

350 g / 12 oz / 1½ cups unsalted butter,
    softened

65 g / 2½ oz / ½ cup unsalted pistachios,
    shelled

75 g / 3 oz / ⅓ cup strawberry jam (jelly)

75 g / 3 oz / ⅓ cup passion fruit purée

METHOD

• Preheat the oven to 180°C (160°C fan) / 350F / gas 4 and grease and line two large baking trays with greaseproof paper.

• Combine 450 g / 1 lb / 4½ cups of icing sugar with the ground almonds in a large mixing bowl.

• Beat the egg whites with a pinch of salt in a separate, clean mixing bowl until stiffly peaked. Fold the egg whites into the ground almond mixture and then divide into six small bowls.

• Add food dye to three of the bowls, leaving a fourth plain. Add 1 tsp of almond extract to the fifth and the cocoa powder to the sixth. Mix well until incorporated. Spoon into six, separate piping bags fitted with round nozzles.

• Pipe eight rounds of each mixture onto the baking trays, spaced apart. Stud the almond macaroons with chopped hazelnuts. Leave them for 15 minutes, and then bake for 8-10 minutes until just set. Remove to a wire rack to cool.

• Heat the cream in a heatproof bowl in the microwave until hot, then add the chocolate and stir until smooth. Set to one side.

• Beat together the butter and remaining icing sugar in a mixing bowl using an electric mixer. Once pale and thick, divide the mixture between four bowls.

• Blitz the pistachios in a food processor until finely ground, and then add to one bowl, stirring well.

• Add the strawberry jam to another bowl and add the passion fruit purée and remaining almond extract to bowls, mixing thoroughly. Spoon the fillings into clean piping bags.

• Pipe the passion fruit buttercream onto the undersides of four orange macaroons. Pipe the almond buttercream onto four of the almond and hazelnut macaroons and pipe the chocolate ganache onto half of the chocolate and plain macaroons.

• Pipe the strawberry buttercream onto the red macaroons and the pistachio buttercream onto the green macaroons. Sandwich the matching halves together, before serving.

Peanut Brittle

Makes: 16 pieces   Preparation time: 2 hours 20 minutes   Cooking time: 15 minutes

INGREDIENTS

225 g / 8 oz / 1 cup caster (superfine) sugar

225 g / 8 oz / 1 ¾ cups salted peanuts

METHOD

- Grease and line an 18 cm (7 in) square baking tin with greaseproof paper.
- Place the sugar in a saucepan set over a medium heat.
- Leave the sugar to dissolve undisturbed until it starts to brown, swirling it gently until it starts to turn amber.
- Cook the sugar until it registers 138°C / 280F on a sugar thermometer.
- Add the peanuts and swirl to coat.
- Continue to cook until the sugar reaches 149°C / 300F.
- Pour into the prepared tin and leave to cool and set for 2 hours.
- Turn out and break into pieces before serving.

Pistachio Nougat

Makes: 32 pieces   Preparation time: 6 hours 15 minutes   Cooking time: 20-25 minutes

INGREDIENTS

275 g / 10 oz / 1 ¼ cups caster (superfine) sugar

55 ml / 2 fl. oz / ¼ cup water

250 g / 9 oz / 1 cup liquid glucose

1 large egg white, at room temperature

200 g / 7 oz / 1 ½ cups pistachios, chopped

100 g / 3 ½ oz / ⅔ cup dried cranberries

1 tsp vanilla extract

METHOD

• Preheat the oven to 160°C (140°C fan) / 325F / gas 3.

• Grease and line a 20 cm x 10 cm x 5 cm (8 in x 4 in x 2 in) baking tin with greaseproof paper.

• Combine the sugar, water and glucose in a saucepan, cooking over a medium heat until the sugar has dissolved.

• Cook until the mixture registers 120°C / 248F on a sugar thermometer.

• Start to beat the egg white in a separate mixing bowl until soft peaks form.

• Once the sugar reaches 136-138°C / 277-280F, remove it from the heat and beat into the egg white in a slow, steady stream until fully incorporated.

• Keep beating for 2-3 minutes until thick and glossy.

• Stir in the pistachios, cranberries and vanilla extract, and then spoon into the tin, levelling the mixture with a wet tablespoon.

• Cover with a sheet of oiled greaseproof paper and gently weigh down.

• Leave the nougat to set for at least 6 hours until firm.

• Once firm, turn out and cut into portions before serving.

Coconut Ice

Makes: 24 pieces   **Preparation time:** 2 hours 25-30 minutes   **Cooking time:** 15 minutes

INGREDIENTS

450 g / 1 lb / 2 cups caster (superfine) sugar

150 ml / 5 fl. oz / ⅔ cup water

¾ tsp vanilla extract

110 g / 4 oz / 1 ½ cups desiccated coconut

a few drops of natural red food dye

METHOD

• Grease and line the base and sides of an 18 cm x 18 cm x 6 cm (7 in x 7 in x 2 ½ in) baking tin with greaseproof paper.

• Combine the sugar and water in a large saucepan set over a medium heat.

• Cook, stirring frequently, until the sugar dissolves.

• Increase the heat and bring the syrup towards boiling until it registers 120°C / 248F on a sugar thermometer.

• Remove the syrup from the heat and stir in the vanilla extract and coconut.

• Continue to beat for 8-10 minutes as it cools and thickens.

• Pour half of the mixture into the prepared tin and spread evenly with a spatula.

• Beat a few drops of dye into the remaining mixture until uniformly pink.

• Pour the pink mixture into the tin and over the other half.

• Spread evenly with the back of a tablespoon and leave to cool for 2 hours until set.

• Turn out the coconut ice, cut into cubes and serve.

Sugared Almonds

Makes: approx. 275 almonds   Preparation time: 1 hour 45-50 minutes   Cooking time: 25-30 minutes

INGREDIENTS

450 g / 1 lb / 2 cups caster (superfine) sugar
150 ml / 5 fl. oz / ⅔ cup water
1 tbsp liquid glucose
350 g / 12 oz / 3 cups blanched almonds
225 ml / 8 fl. oz / 1 cup clear piping gel
a few drops of natural yellow food dye
a few drops of natural pink food dye
a few drops of natural green food dye
a few drops of natural orange food dye

METHOD

• Combine the sugar and water in a saucepan set over a medium heat until the sugar dissolves.

• Stir in the glucose and continue to cook until the syrup registers 115°C / 240F on a sugar thermometer.

• Remove the syrup from the heat and leave until the bubbles subside.

• Place a silicone mat on a large rimmed baking tray and pour the syrup onto it, letting it spread out.

• Leave it to set until cool enough to handle.

• Use a wooden spoon to bring the piece of fondant into a ball, kneading it until smooth and white in appearance.

• Place the rolled out fondant on a tray and cover with a damp tea towel, leaving it to rest for 1 hour.

• After an hour, knead again for a few minutes.

• Line a large baking tray with greaseproof paper and set to one side.

• Melt the fondant in a saucepan set over a medium-low heat.

• Dip the almonds into the melted fondant, then pick them out with a fork and leave them to dry and harden on the greaseproof paper.

• Turn over the almonds after five minutes and leave them to dry out completely.

• Divide the piping gel between four small bowls and dye each with the various food dyes.

• Once the coated almonds are dry, paint their exteriors with the gels, giving them more than one coat if necessary.

• Let the almonds dry out overnight before serving.

Marzipan Fruits

Makes: 40 fruits   Preparation time: 2-3 hours   Cooking time: 10 minutes

INGREDIENTS

175 ml / 6 fl. oz / ¾ cup double (heavy) cream

2 tbsp unsalted butter

200 g / 7 oz / 1 ⅓ cups dark chocolate, chopped

3 digestive biscuits, crushed

65 g / 2 ½ oz / ½ cup icing (confectioners') sugar, sifted

600 g / 1 lb 2 oz / 3 cups marzipan, room temperature

55 g / 2 oz / ⅔ cup desiccated coconut

110 ml / 4 fl. oz / ½ cup clear piping gel

liquid food dye (red and green)

110 g / 4 oz / ½ cup granulated sugar

a small handful of cloves

METHOD

• Place the cream and butter in a heatproof bowl sat over a half-filled saucepan of simmering water.

• Warm until the cream is hot and then remove the bowl from the heat, stirring in the chocolate until melted.

• Add the crushed biscuits and stir again to incorporate.

• Let the mixture cool and thicken, then cover and chill for 1 hour until firm but not set.

• Remove from the fridge and roll tablespoons of the mixture into truffles between your palms.

• Roll the truffles in icing sugar, coating them evenly, and place them in paper cases.

• Set to one side to dry.

• Break off pieces of marzipan and shape into apples and strawberries between your hands; use real fruit as a visual guide.

• Shape more marzipan into round balls between your palms.

• Roll in the coconut to coat and place them in paper cases.

• Divide the decorating gel into two small bowls. Add 1-2 drops of food dye to each bowl and stir to blend.

• Brush the bodies of the fruit with dye, building up the colour with layers.

• Let the dye dry before rolling the fruit in granulated sugar.

• Craft the cloves into stems, placing them in the top of the apples and strawberries.

• Shape any remaining marzipan into leaves and colour green with food dye.

• Place the fruit in cases and serve alongside the coconut marzipan and the truffles.

Nutty French Nougat

Makes: 32 pieces   Preparation time: 4 hours 20-25 minutes   Cooking time: 20-25 minutes

INGREDIENTS

375 g / 13 oz / 1 ⅔ cups caster (superfine)
  sugar

2 tbsp liquid glucose

110 ml / 4 fl. oz / ½ cup water

350 g / 12 oz / 1 ½ cups honey

2 medium egg whites

100 g / 3 ½ oz / ⅔ cup candied mixed fruit,
  chopped

100 g / 3 ½ oz / ¾ cup almonds, toasted

75 g / 3 oz / ½ cup hazelnuts (cobnuts), toasted

75 g / 3 oz / ⅔ cup flaked (slivered)
  almonds, toasted

75 g / 3 oz / ⅔ cup shelled pistachios

a pinch of salt

2 tbsp butter, diced

110 ml / 4 fl. oz / ½ cup clear piping gel

liquid food dye (red, yellow, green, brown)

METHOD

• Line an 18 cm (7 in) square baking tin with rice paper.

• Combine 350 g / 12 oz / 1 ½ cups of sugar with the liquid glucose and the water in a saucepan set over a medium heat.

• Cook steadily until the sugar dissolves, continuing to cook until it registers 143°C / 290F on a sugar thermometer.

• Warm the honey in a separate pan until just bubbling, and then add the syrup, cooking it until it comes back up to 143°C / 290F.

• Whisk the egg whites and remaining sugar with an electric whisk in a large mixing bowl until stiffly peaked.

• Slowly pour in the hot honey syrup, whisking constantly. Continue whisking for 5 minutes until thick and glossy.

• Stir in the candied fruits, nuts and salt, and then stir in the butter until thoroughly combined.

• Spoon into the tin and smooth the top. Cover with more rice paper and press down gently to level the surface.

• Leave the nougat to set at room temperature for 4 hours.

• Turn out of the tin and cut into squares.

• Divide the decorating gel into four small bowls. Add 1-2 drops of food dye to each bowl and stir to blend.

• Brush the squares with the gels and leave to dry before serving.

DOWN MEMORY LANE

LUXURY
CHOCOLATES

White & Milk Chocolate Truffles

Makes: 60 truffles   Preparation time: 55-60 minutes   Cooking time: 20 minutes

INGREDIENTS

650 ml / 1 pint 4 fl. oz / 2 ⅔ cups double (heavy) cream

55 g / 2 oz / ¼ cup unsalted butter, cubed

450 g / 1 lb / 3 cups milk chocolate, chopped

450 g / 1 lb / 3 cups white chocolate, chopped

100 g / 3 ½ oz / ⅔ cup cocoa powder

75 g / 3 oz / 1 cup desiccated coconut

55 g / 2 oz / ⅓ cup dark chocolate, chopped

METHOD

- Warm the cream and butter in a saucepan set over a moderate heat.

- Place the milk chocolate in a heatproof bowl and set it to one side. Place 200 g / 7 oz / 1 ⅓ cup of white chocolate in another heatproof bowl.

- As the cream approaches boiling point, remove it from the heat and pour two-thirds over the milk chocolate and the rest over the white.

- Leave them to sit for a minute before stirring until evenly melted. Cover and chill both mixtures for 20 minutes until firm.

- Roll two-thirds of the milk chocolate mixture into balls, arranging them on a baking tray lined with greaseproof paper. With the remaining mixture, roll tablespoons into rough truffle shapes and place on the tray.

- Roll the white chocolate mixture into balls and arrange on a separate lined tray to chill. Temper the remaining white chocolate and then place in a food processor and blitz until it resembles breadcrumbs.

- Meanwhile, fill a large bowl with boiling water and set it to one side.

- Scrape down the sides of the processor bowl and continue to blitz for a further 1-2 minutes until the chocolate starts to clump into a ball. Break up the ball with a spatula and scrape it down into the base of the bowl.

- Blitz the chocolate again until it starts to liquefy and reaches 30°C / 87F on a sugar thermometer.

- Pour the water out of the warm bowl and dry it thoroughly. Scrape the liquid chocolate into the warmed bowl and stir until even and fluid.

- Use a skewer to pick up half of the round milk chocolate truffles and dip them into the melted chocolate. Once coated evenly, arrange on a baking tray lined with greaseproof paper. Chill for 15 minutes.

- Roll the remaining milk truffle balls in cocoa powder and leave them to dry.

- Drizzle any remaining melted white chocolate over the rough truffles and leave them to dry.

- Roll the white chocolate truffle balls in the desiccated coconut and set to one side.

- Melt the dark chocolate in a small heatproof bowl set over a half-filled saucepan of simmering water, stirring occasionally. Drizzle the melted chocolate over the coated white truffles and leave them to set. Serve the truffles in paper cases.

Champagne Truffles

Makes: 24 of each   Preparation time: 1 hour 30 minutes   Cooking time: 15-20 minutes

INGREDIENTS

350 ml / 12 fl. oz / 1 ½ cups pink sparkling wine or Champagne

110 ml / 4 fl. oz / ½ cup double (heavy) cream

750 g / 1 lb 10 oz / 5 cups white chocolate, chopped

2 tsp powdered raspberry jelly

55 g / 2 oz / ¼ cup granulated sugar

1 tsp vanilla extract

1 tbsp unsalted butter

METHOD

- Place the sparkling wine in a saucepan and warm over a moderate heat until reduced to approximately 1 tbsp in volume.

- Place a heatproof bowl over a saucepan of gently simmering water.

- Add the reduced wine and half of the cream, warming until combined and hot.

- Add half of the chocolate gradually, whisking until melted and smooth.

- Sprinkle over the powdered jelly and mix with a spatula until combined. As the mixture thickens, remove any cocoa butter that rises to the top.

- Cover the bowl and chill for 10 minutes until firm.

- Scoop out the truffle mixture between your palms into small balls and then roll in the granulated sugar.

- Arrange the truffles on a lined baking tray, cover loosely and chill.

- Place a clean, heatproof bowl over a saucepan of gently simmering water.

- Add the vanilla extract, butter and the remaining cream, warming them until hot. Gradually whisk in the remaining chocolate.

- Once smooth, cover the bowl and chill for 15 minutes until firm but not hard.

- Scoop out the mixture and roughly roll into balls between your palms.

- Run the tines of a fork over the truffles before arranging them on a lined baking tray.

- Chill for 1 hour until set. Serve alongside the pink champagne truffles in cases.

Mint Chocolate Truffles

Makes: 32 truffles   Preparation time: 3 hours   Cooking time: 5-10 minutes

INGREDIENTS

250 ml / 9 fl. oz / 1 cup double (heavy) cream
450 g / 1 lb / 3 cups dark chocolate, chopped
½ tsp peppermint extract
150 g / 5 oz / 1 cup cocoa powder
a few sprigs of mint, to garnish

METHOD

+ Heat the cream in a saucepan until it starts to boil.

+ Remove the pan from the heat and add the chocolate, leaving it to sit untouched for 1 minute.

+ Add the peppermint extract and stir until the chocolate and cream are melted together and smooth.

+ Cover and chill the mixture for 45 minutes until firm but not set.

+ Take small scoops of the mixture and roll into truffles.

+ Roll the truffles in cocoa powder before arranging on a lined baking tray.

+ Chill for 2 hours until set.

+ Roll in more cocoa powder if desired before serving with a garnish of mint leaves.

Chocolate Orange Truffles

Makes: 24 truffles   Preparation time: 45-50 minutes   Cooking time: 10 minutes

INGREDIENTS

300 g / 10 ½ oz / 2 cups dark chocolate, chopped
150 ml / 5 fl. oz / ⅔ cup double (heavy) cream
2 tbsp orange liqueur
½ tsp vanilla extract
100 g / 3 ½ oz / ⅔ cup cocoa powder

METHOD

• Place the chocolate in a heatproof bowl and set it to one side.

• Warm the cream in a saucepan until it starts to boil.

• Remove the cream from the heat and pour over the chocolate. Let it sit for a minute, then add the liqueur and vanilla extract, stirring until smooth.

• Cover and chill for 20-25 minutes until firm but not set.

• Take scoops of the mixture and shape roughly into truffles.

• Arrange them on a tray lined with greaseproof paper and chill for 15 minutes.

• Roll the truffles in cocoa powder and leave to dry at room temperature before serving.

Chocolate Candied Peels

Makes: approx. 40   Preparation time: 2 hours 20 minutes   Cooking time: 45 minutes

INGREDIENTS

4 large oranges, washed

225 g / 8 oz / 1 cup caster (superfine) sugar

225 ml / 8 fl. oz / 1 cup water

300 g / 10 ½ oz / 2 cups dark chocolate, chopped

METHOD

- Use a vegetable peeler to pare the zest from the oranges.
- Remove as much of the white pith from the zest as possible, then cut the zest into 0.5 cm (¼ in) wide strips.
- Cook the strips of zest in a saucepan of simmering water for 10 minutes.
- Drain well and set them to one side.
- Combine the equal amounts of sugar and water in a heavy-based saucepan.
- Cook over a medium heat until the sugar has dissolved and a syrup forms.
- Add the strips of orange zest and gently simmer them in the syrup for 30 minutes until soft and translucent.
- Line a large baking tray or wire rack with a sheet of greaseproof paper and lift the strips of zest onto the paper.
- Leave the peels to cool and dry until tacky to the touch; 1 hour.
- Melt the chocolate in a heatproof bowl set atop a half-filled saucepan of simmering water.
- Stir occasionally until the chocolate has melted and remove the bowl from the heat.
- Dip half of the peels into the melted chocolate before returning them to the greaseproof paper to set.
- Chill the chocolate and plain peels for 1 hour before serving.

Chocolate-coated Coffee Beans

Makes: approx. 200 beans   Preparation time: 2 hours 15 minutes   Cooking time: 10 minutes

INGREDIENTS

225 g / 8 oz / 1 ½ cups coffee beans
450 g / 1 lb / 3 cups dark chocolate, chopped

METHOD

- Preheat the oven to 180°C (200°C fan) / 350F / gas 4 and line a large baking tray with a sheet of greaseproof paper or a silicone mat.
- Arrange the coffee beans on a baking tray in a single layer and roast for 10 minutes.
- Remove to a wire rack to cool.
- Place the chocolate in a food processor and blitz until it resembles breadcrumbs.
- Meanwhile, fill a large bowl with boiling water and set to one side.
- Scrape down the sides of the food processor bowl and continue to blitz for a further 2 minutes until the chocolate starts to clump into a ball.
- Break up the ball with a spatula and scrape it down into the base of the bowl.
- Blitz the chocolate again until it starts to liquefy and register 32°C / 90F on a sugar thermometer.
- Pour the water out of the warm bowl and dry it thoroughly. Scrape the liquid chocolate into the warmed bowl and stir until even and fluid.
- Add a third of the beans and stir to coat before using a pair of kitchen tweezers to arrange them on the tray.
- Repeat with the remaining beans, spacing them apart on the tray when coated.
- As they set, roll them carefully between your palms to smooth their edges.
- Leave them to set for 2 hours before serving.

White Chocolate Rose Creams

Makes: 24   Preparation time: 3 hours 15-20 minutes   Cooking time: 5-10 minutes

INGREDIENTS

175 ml / 6 fl. oz / ¾ cup double (heavy) cream

500 g / 1 lb 2 oz / 3 ⅓ cups white chocolate, chopped

55 g / 2 oz / ¼ cup unsalted butter, cut into small pieces

2-3 tsp rose water

75 g / 3 oz / 1 cup desiccated coconut

a few drops of natural red food dye

METHOD

• Heat the cream in a pan until it reaches boiling point. Immediately remove from the heat.

• Place the chocolate and butter in a bowl and pour over the hot cream.

• Gently whisk until the mixture is smooth and allow it to cool. Stir in the rose water.

• Cover the bowl and chill for about 3 hours until firm, but not hard.

• Put half the coconut into a small bowl and stir in a little red food dye, mixing well until evenly coated.

• Put the remaining coconut into another bowl.

• Use 1 tsp to scoop a ball from the chocolate and roll it between your hands until it is round.

• Roll the truffle in the red and white coconut until covered.

• Repeat with the remaining chocolate and coconut. Chill until ready to serve.

Dark Chocolate Slab

Serves: 6-8   Preparation time: 1 hour 10 minutes   Cooking time: 10-15 minutes

INGREDIENTS

450 g / 1 lb / 3 cups 80% cocoa solids dark chocolate

125 g / 4 ½ oz / 1 cup un-blanched whole almonds

a small handful of coffee beans

5 cm (2 in) piece of cinnamon stick

METHOD

• Grease and line the sides of an 18 cm (7 in) square baking tin with greaseproof paper.

• Melt the chocolate in a heatproof bowl set atop a half-filled saucepan of simmering water.

• Stir occasionally until the chocolate has melted, and keep the bowl over the saucepan, turning the heat off underneath the water.

• Blitz the almonds in a food processor until finely ground.

• Crush the coffee beans and cinnamon stick in a mortar and pestle.

• Pour the melted chocolate into the prepared tin and sprinkle over the finely ground almonds.

• Top with the crushed coffee beans and cinnamon before chilling for 1 hour until set.

• Turn out the chocolate before breaking into pieces and serving.

Nutritional Information

Recipe name	Makes	Calories/sweet (kcal)	Fat (g)	Saturated Fat (g)
Almond Hearts	48	107	4.3	0.3
Berry Jellies	150	22	0	0
Butterscotch Fudge	32	80	4.6	3.2
Candied Fruit	60	35	0	0
Caramel Chews	48	59	2.9	1.8
Cassis Cream Fudge	24	90	1.3	0.8
Champagne Truffles	24	105	6.1	3.7
Chocolate & Coconut Fudge	32	135	4.9	3.1
Chocolate & Vanilla Fudge	48	81	4.5	2.8
Chocolate Candied Peels	40	39	0.7	0.4
Chocolate-coated Coffee Beans	200	11	0.7	0.4
Chocolate-coated Honeycomb	16	223	8.4	4
Chocolate Orange Truffles	24	57	4.4	2.7
Coconut Ice	24	96	1.6	1.4
Dark Chocolate Slab	16	97	7.4	2.3
French Macaroons	60	203	12.67	4.53
Fruit & Nut Florentines	24	181	11.5	5.26
Fruit Jellies	200	20	0	0
Gum Drops	80	36	0	0
Jelly Beans	120	8	0	0
Lemon Drops	24	50	0	0
Liquorice Sticks	32	96	3.2	2
Marshmallows	120	20	0.1	0
Marzipan Fruits	40	115	7.5	2.5
Mint Chocolate Truffles	32	63	5.3	3.2
Nutty French Nougat	32	154	6	0.8
Orange, Lemon & Lime Drops	48	71	0	0
Peanut Brittle	16	140	7.5	1.1
Peanut Butter Fudge	32	175	11.5	4.9
Peppermint Candy Cane	16	121	0	0
Peppermint Creams	32	87	0.8	0.5
Pistachio Nougat	32	110	2.8	0.3
Rhubarb Custards	60	30	0	0
Salted Butter Toffees	48	47	2	1.3
Salted Caramels	12	214	13.7	8.5
Seaside Rock Lollies	16	128	0	0
Soft Nougat Squares	16	112	0.3	0.2
Strawberry Laces	24	29	0	0
Sugared Almonds	275	16	0.8	0
Toffee	16	134	8.9	5.6
Turkish Delight	32	80	0	0
Vanilla Tablet	32	110	1.8	1.2
White and Milk Chocolate Truffles	60	170	10.19	6.07
White Chocolate Rose Creams	24	145	12.3	7.9

Cholesterol (mg)	Sodium (mg)	Carbs (g)	Fibre (g)	Sugars (g)	Protein (g)
0	4.4	14.9	0.5	13.5	1.9
0	0	5.6	0	5.3	0
8.1	1.1	4.9	0	4.8	0
0	0	8.8	0.1	8.7	0
9.6	8.5	8.6	0	8.3	0.1
4.8	3	20	0	19.9	0.3
6	15.7	10.8	0	10.7	1
7.6	34.6	20	0.7	19.7	2.3
13.9	3.3	10.3	0	10.1	0.3
0	0	8.2	0.5	7.6	0.24
0.3	0	1.1	0.2	0.9	0.2
6.5	179.6	35.2	0.9	33	2.1
8.6	3.3	4.5	1.9	2.1	1.2
0	12	20.9	0.2	20.7	0.1
0	0.1	6.1	2.4	4.5	2.3
15.7	15.97	20.67	1.44	18	2.7
14.1	8.71	18.5	1.52	14.61	2.2
0	1.9	4.3	0	4.2	0.7
0	4.9	9.1	0	9	0.3
0.4	0	1.1	0	1.1	0
0	0	12.1	0	12	0
8.6	21.8	14.5	0	12.3	0.6
0	0	4.7	0	4.3	0.1
2.4	13	11.1	1	8.6	1.7
10.7	4	4.9	2.1	2.1	1.4
1.6	14.3	23.8	1.3	23.3	2.3
0	0	19	0	19	0
0	58	16.6	1	14.6	3.5
15.1	46.7	16.2	0.8	15.3	2.7
0	0	31.5	0	31.4	0
2.5	11.4	19.5	0	19.3	0.8
0	1.8	20.5	0.8	18.8	1.4
0	0.03	7.77	0	7.8	0
6.9	72.9	7.3	0	7.2	0
47.2	56.4	22.8	1	22.3	0.8
0	0.1	32.8	0	32.7	0
0	17.2	26.5	0	26	0.7
0	1.1	6.9	0	6.9	0.5
0	0	2	0.2	1.8	0.3
23.5	1.2	14.1	0	14.1	0.1
0	0.5	20.5	0	15.9	0
5.5	16.4	22.8	0	22.8	1.2
19.6	20.53	10.82	0.89	9.00	1.62
17.9	29.9	14	0.1	13.7	1.5

Index